VOW

CLEVELAND STATE UNIVERSITY POETRY CENTER
NEW POETRY

Michael Dumanis, Series Editor

Samuel Amadon, *The Hartford Book*
John Bradley, *You Don't Know What You Don't Know*
Lily Brown, *Rust or Go Missing*
Elyse Fenton, *Clamor*
Emily Kendal Frey, *The Grief Performance*
Rebecca Hazelton, *Vow*
Rebecca Gayle Howell, *Render / An Apocalypse*
Dora Malech, *Say So*
Shane McCrae, *Mule*
Helena Mesa, *Horse Dance Underwater*
Philip Metres, *To See the Earth*
Zach Savich, *The Firestorm*
Sandra Simonds, *Mother Was a Tragic Girl*
S. E. Smith, *I Live in a Hut*
Mathias Svalina, *Destruction Myth*
Allison Titus, *Sum of Every Lost Ship*
Liz Waldner, *Trust*
Allison Benis White, *Self-Portrait with Crayon*
William D. Waltz, *Adventures in the Lost Interiors of America*
Jon Woodward, *Uncanny Valley*
Wendy Xu, *You Are Not Dead*

For a complete listing of titles please visit
www.csuohio.edu/poetrycenter

VOW

REBECCA HAZELTON

Cleveland State University Poetry Center / Cleveland, Ohio

ISBN 978-0-9860257-0-9

First edition

17   16   15   14   13   5   4   3   2   1

This book is published by the Cleveland State University Poetry Center,
2121 Euclid Avenue, Cleveland, Ohio 44115-2214
www.csuohio.edu/poetrycenter and is distributed by
SPD / Small Press Distribution, Inc. www.spdbooks.org.

Cover image: Mark Stafford
Book cover design: Windham Graves in Archivo Black and Eau
Vow was designed and typeset by Amy Freels in ITC Slimbach, with Helvetica
Neue display.

LIBRARY OF CONGRESS CATALOGING-IN-PUBLICATION DATA
Hazelton, Rebecca, 1978–
  Vow / Rebecca Hazelton. — First edition.
    pages cm
  ISBN 978-0-9860257-0-9 (pbk. : alk. paper)
  I. Title.
  PS3608.A9884V69 2013
  811'.6—dc23
                          2012051265

ACKNOWLEDGMENTS

"Book of Memory" and "Book of Forget" were first published in *Agni*.

"Book of Excess" was first published in the web journal *Anti—*.

"Fox and Rabbit Go to the Movies," "Fox Undresses Rabbit," and "Fox Dresses Rabbit" were first published in *Barn Owl Review*.

"Elise Qua Elise" was first published in the web journal *Everyday Genius*.

"Springtime, Elise, and You're Missing All of It," and "Elise as Marie Antoinette at Her Toilette" were first published in *Gettysburg Review*.

"Fairness Doesn't Enter In" was first published in the online literary review *Jet Fuel Review*.

"Elise, Your Phone Is Ringing" and "What Elise Means to Me" were first published in the web journal *Juked*.

"Elise Enters the House of Triumph," "Revision: Elise," "Elise is Not Atlanta or Atalanta," and "On First Sleeping With Elise in the Presence of My Ex-Husband" were first published in *Pank*.

"Dear Chanel, Dear Alabama, Dear Elise" was first published in *Phoebe*.

"Book of Absence" was first published in *Pleiades*.

"Elise as Android at the Japan! Culture + Hyperculture Festival" was first published in *Rattle*.

"Not Here to Buy The Leopard" and "My Answer to You Is Yes (Formerly No)" were first published in *Smartish Pace*.

"Love Poem for What Is" was first published in *The Southeast Review*.

"Questions About the Wife" and "Those Horses" were first published in *The Southern Review*.

"Questions About the Wife" was featured on *Verse Daily*.

"Book of Janus" was selected for *Best New Poets 2011: 50 Poems from Emerging Writers*, edited by D. A. Powell, Jazzy Danziger, and Jeb Livingood.

"Book of Forget" was selected for *Best American Poetry 2013* by guest editor Denise Duhamel.

"Gold Empire" was first published as a winner of the 2012 "Discovery" / *Boston Review* Poetry Contest sponsored by the 92Y Unterberg Poetry Center in partnership with the *Boston Review*.

Special thanks to the University of Wisconsin's Institute for Creative Writing for awarding me a Jay C. and Ruth Halls Fellowship and to the Vermont Studio Center for awarding me a VSC Fellowship.

Thanks to Mark Stafford, Matt Guenette, Frank Giampietro, Sandra Simonds, Sean Bishop, Kara Candito, Brittany Cavallaro, Laurel Bastian, Ron Wallace, Jay Robinson, Jimin Seo, Nancy Reddy, Amaud Johnson, Jacques Rancourt, and Yuko Sakata for reading and commenting on many of these poems. Thanks to Michael Dumanis for selecting this book.

CONTENTS

VOW

BOOK OF MEMORY

In my seeing there was a blank and he filled that blank
with words, there were words for darkness which made it lift,
there were words for cover which ripped them off,
there were legs that crossed and hearts that crossed,
promises red and read, and the pluck of banjo had a name
for that twang, and the way he called the world into notice,
that had a word, too. Once I saw I couldn't unsee
and the worst was that the light glaring from the letters
left blue haze under my eyelids. There are no photographs
of this time, and I can only go by what others
tell me: I was blurred and erratic, I drew a circle
of white chalk around me and called myself inviolate,
I watched for horses on the horizon, my walls
were under siege from smaller men who called themselves
heroes. They say I reached over the balustrade and picked
up the tiny ships and threw them over the edge of the world.
I tore my hair, cut one breast from my body and plattered it
as around my fortifications one man pulled another man
behind his chariot. If they say that's how I was,
that's how I was. I have no words for the one in the mirror
who apes me every morning. She's not the one I remember
imagining as a young girl. There must be a way to unsee
how I tap the glass and she taps back, and which wall,
which Cassandra weeping—everything I saw I spoke to his ear,
and the wall crashed into place between us, the horse
had a bellyful of it, the blank was full of small soldiers,
and he turned from my beauty and said my name.

THE PASTORAL IS DIFFICULT

In winter it won't seed or pop
in the banked gray snow the pastoral
can't canter little sheep can't low
to the stars sweet bovine eyes
the shepherd who asks for his love
to stay doesn't have a good health plan
the girl is fickle and wants
the pastoral but she also wants

       a house where the sheep can't barge in
       a crown made of metal not primrose
       the shepherd to be a shepherd
       at night but also a stock analyst

the pastoral is difficult
in winter when the spring
won't pop up when the book lies flat
when the rain is sleet when the goats'
horizontal pupils the world so slender
when the difficult is the everyday
is the song he plays out on the pipes
but when that won't do he has a record
he has a cd an mp3 he can sing this song
forever the same tenor the same words
and the pasture is of the past the animals
are stacked and penned the pigs' tails
are clipped because they are confined
and mad and gnaw at their fellows
and the homogenized chickens
and the mechanized eggs the pastoral
sheeted with ice
he says come live with me
and there are pleasures
but whether they can be found
is difficult to say

QUESTIONS ABOUT THE WIFE

I'm having trouble understanding the wife.
The wife seems like she is only there as a foil to your actions.
I want to know how the wife feels when you drag her
and your son down into the basement to start a new religion.
The religion has something to do with cowering
before a force greater than yourself and then being buried alive.
I want to know how the wife behaves in small, enclosed spaces:
if she is trying to comfort your son by telling him Daddy likes
to play funny games, or if she is already visualizing
herself walking into a women's shelter, your son
on her back and maybe, because this is a fantasy,
she carries a burning torch, like an angry villager, or a goddess.
Does the wife merit any revenge after you weed whack
the coffee table? Does she agree with you that the coffee table
is yours to destroy because you built it? What has she built
in the house that is hers to destroy? What kind of childhood
has the wife endured that allows her to understand you?
In her past life or lives, was the wife ever a shepherdess?
Does she see you as a sort of Pan, goatish, and pricked
by ticks, but also very well-endowed? When the wife transforms
into a tree can she still think or is she just a green haze
inside, an idea of growing? I would like to see the wife
peel off that bark, leaving only enough for modesty's sake,
although as this is your poem, we can take a bit more off.
I want to see her uproot herself, pick up the house and shake it.
How many people fall out?
The wife has something about her the Germans
would call *unheimlich*. I sometimes catch a glimpse of the wife
out of the corner of my eye but then I look away.
I cannot look directly at the wife. The wife is a conflagration
of everything dear. I wonder sometimes if she is faking;
There is a certain note she holds too long

so the orgasm is more operatic, less genuine.

When she cries, *Oh my God*, really, she should stutter.

Let's say the wife wakes up in the morning.

You have already made breakfast. Does your kindness feel oppressive?

Does she want to take your weed whacker through the house?

Has she ever, in a fit of anger, destroyed your pornography?

When you found a picture of the wife online with a foreign handprint

smacked red on her ass, how quickly did your shock turn to arousal?

Are you aware the wife is breaking down in public places,

and sometimes cannot move for thirty minutes? Sometimes

her arm goes entirely numb from the shoulder down. I think the wife

might need some fine-tuning, some elbow grease,

some wrenching apart, and then reassembling.

I AM NOT ATLANTA,
WE'RE NOT ATLANTIS

Some days I'm the ocean. Some days a bathtub.
Either way, you're enormous.
Your knees

> an archipelago to your toes' atoll.

Though you're not half a city or even a suburb,

> you are fabled.

Roads do lead in, roads do

> sulk out.

There's a fountain that pulses,

> but it's not a heart,

and this isn't empathy, either.

So later, there's foam on your feet.

> So later, you are standing

on a cord of seaweed.

The sand that slips
around your heels as the sea pulls

> does what it can,
> but you have your own momentum.

Your intended

> is a fire farther down shore,

but she's not me

> burning or otherwise.

BOOK OF ABSENCE

Darling, the forest is disappearing. Not the one you remember, with the little girl and her basket and the wolf astride, but the one that surrounded your small house as a child and was smaller than you realized: the forest you planned to run into and never out of if someone didn't understand you, and soon.

Darling, we have been talking overmuch, and the forest is disappearing faster. The few trees aren't trees but cellphone towers, disguised, blunting the beaks of woodpeckers. When I spoke to you in the middle of the night, the dream was that I was lying next to you. Our talks tunneled through a phone line like it was 1989 but now wing through the air and mingle with others, just as everyday, as unspecial. The forest once covered all of England but sailed away. The forest had a peacock farm inside it and far off calls, but now a pig farm, now a lake of pig shit, now a green and dying bloom.

Darling, while we have been talking at night when I thought you were someone else, the forest has reassessed its options. While the little girl weighed her basket for options the wolf worried over the forest's stitch, and the whole thing came undone. While you were dreaming the forest a dream of the green bloom of the earth, I dreamed a conversation I wanted to hear, to overhear how you've

been dreaming me as a girl in the woods, the
trees coming down all around her, when the
forest, the forest wakes up and the cellphones
all ring.

ELISE ENTERS THE HOUSE OF TRIUMPH

When I try to talk
           about the past, it becomes a jaguar throw
                         wrapped around
                your bare shoulders,
illegal plush, musky repulse,
while you, imperious and resolute, smoke
           from a cigarette holder—
        Dahling, stop your whining.

              Jukebox jewel, princess cut,
      you were a libretto sung into the smut
           of The Claremont Lounge,
a bit of shining glass
           wedged between pleather cushions.

Meth gave you cheekbones
           to die for, whipped away the alcoholic plump,
           and burnished you
to a brief golden glamour.

        You posed in black and white,
           your breasts billowing to the camera,
      lips parted, Marilyning with the best of them.

        O, I have all the time now
                to listen
to your proclamations,
           and you have all the time to make them—
if there is one last story you'd like
           to star in, to shine again
              like a tinfoil tiara,

just say, and I'll write you
                    a final triumph
over friends like me, who disappeared
            into smug sobriety, the snug safety
of a circadian life—

            I hear you were still
an unapologetic blonde, Dahling,
                I hear your final word was *No.*

THOSE HORSES

When the children disembarked from the ferry and stepped as a group
onto the sandy shore, no one wearing flip-flops due to the cold,
and the sea below as gray as the sea above, it was clear
the fog was unexpected, the teachers were nervous; it was clear
the horse splayed on the beach was also unexpected,
the brown seaweed surrounding it like extra strokes from an absent
brush, the belly much larger than those of the horses the children had seen
on television, or at an uncle's farm; the belly was swollen, and one boy
thought it had a foal curled inside, it was tight, and one girl
thought the horse might be sleeping; but how to gather the children,
the teachers asked each other, eye blink to eye blink, let us go
see the grandfather oaks, the oldest trees, they said, let us wander
the crumbling plantation, whose owner spent summers in the north
with his mulatto slave, Elizabeth, and sent their six children
to fine schools, yet the cotton was still picked and shipped,
the slave girls walked with baskets of laundry on their heads,
and there are twenty-four chimneys from twenty-four slave cabins
remaining in three parallel rows, sinking into the sand.
There's something wrong with that horse, one child says,
and the others nod, there was something wrong, there was,
and the teacher said the horses were feral,
descendants of shipwrecks swum ashore, of horses abandoned
by Spanish explorers, of pleasure horses for pretty women
light skinned enough to fuck. But the teachers didn't say that.
They said the horses were beautiful and the horses were a foreign invader,
ripping up the grasses anchoring dunes, ripping out the seams of the island
so more and more washed away, and the horses were our horses
and the horse on the beach wasn't dead but sleeping, look,
there's its mate nuzzling its slack flank, its swollen belly and still neck,
that horse can't be dead or why would its mate stay. Get up, horse, walk away.

SIGNALS FROM THE UNIVERSE

On earth as it is in heaven, the pale forms
motion through the pale day,
                    the snow plow scrapes the gray
from the freezing asphalt,

                    the coffee of the morning
is the steaming engine to the morning,

                              and the ideal is somewhere,
            snow and the ideal plow for it is somewhere,
but not here.
                    Here there is skin and the sleep
that fills it, hair and the hands that part it,
            coats dragged through
                        snow dragged through
            exhaust dragged through
                        air which is ideal
            for life on earth,
                                  but cold today, here it is cold,
here are raccoon tracks, here bicycles, their baskets
            stuffed with hard snow,

                        here bodies
turn in the luxurious heat
                        of heated apartments,
bodies which have hair which have skin
turning in the luxury
                of the other's heat,
and nothing to indicate
            I have been here before,
                        but the print of my boot,
            the signature I left when I crossed

the land bridge

                  to come here

to a pale version

             of my promised glory,

one where gods walk among

                the smallest of us

where an ideal blade

             scrapes the cheek

of the earth.

BOOK OF LONGING

A hair
    —yours—
        swims loose from my own,
    catches on my fingers
        like a comma seeking a pause,
          then disappears down the shower drain
    with the day's sweat and stink.

In the space of these ten minutes,
    the water turning clockwise
        in accordance with the law,

rightness manifests,
and I feel I've come loose
    from this cycle.
Here the hand that acts
remains,
is clean—

        but there have been a torrent of women
        each curtained like me
        and discretely naked,
hidden
in a liquid sheath,
        their fists clenched and mouths cursing
        into the steam, all of them recalling
        the last chaste kiss
        bestowed to the crown of their heads—

the hand that remains
is clean but lacks a reason to unwind
    a binding tangle.

The hand closes, opens, once more,
        and the water sluices the day
                from the hand which is only
        a hand: not a chance, or reprieve, or a door.

I LOVE HIS PROFILE

Let me imagine
                there's no progress,
                        that you do not persist
after I have left the room,
                and let me ignore
                        the selfishness
                        that thought reflects
        as I ignore
        the unflattering world,
the stirrup pants,
dark lipstick,
and introspection.

Let you be ageless.
Let the same image return
                        for each search,
                the same blank face
in the same white room.
Let all the internet mourn
                for lack of you.

I have seen the construction
                on I-80 through Gary, Indiana,
and I have stuttered
                through those ill-marked doglegs,
                        the tumbleweeds on fire,
                        the green fog that descends
                        like the menacing illumination
                                from a spaceship
                                with dubious intent.

There were ponies in the fields
searching for grass in the acres of snow,

their winter coats
shaggy and Miocene,
                and I wondered if somewhere
                            there was a sugar cube for me.
                            Yes, I said it.

But I'm not searching for sweetness
                            or to hear your voice
recorded on a small black box
                    dredged
                    from the wreckage,
                although probably,
if I heard my name, I'd turn.

WHAT ELISE MEANS TO ME

That a heel feels a double needle.
That the gold leaf flaked from her breast
      and settled on my lashes.
That I opened my mouth and there was no music.

     Oh, be quiet, she'd say.
I'm only on the step behind you.
Every day you ascend to the glory
               of your apartment.
It's no tragedy that you turn and I return to another.

That I couldn't sing her back.
That she would rather run to the Midwest
and the promise of limitless plains
than be goated on the wedding table
smeared with butter amongst the mounded grapes,
the ants the ants and their small voices.

That she coolly appraised me and found me wanting.
That my hand would wave to her even as she turned away.

Finally, that these are the veils.
Overlay and inlay, the words
     cover and the words real
the real. *Why wave,* she'd ask.
               It's forever or it's nothing.

FOX AND RABBIT GO TO THE MOVIES

This is nice, isn't it? I like these seats.
How far back we sit. I can't tell when the real movie starts
or if the house burning on screen is a preview
for how the house burns down later. Then a man tumbles out,
and sometimes you are a man, or in a man shape. You wear it
until it wears you. Take my hand and hold it or else
I get dizzy. That's not my hand. Remember
how we searched each other's palms for fortune?
Mine are almost blank. This is nice. The shape
of your shadow has teeth. Later we'll play the game
where I hunt you down and kill you. I'm kidding.
When you talk over the dialogue I can pretend
you're the lead. Tomorrow might be like today
but this room won't be so dark. There are periods
of darkness and of light. In between, the trash
is swept away and our bodies vacate and the seat cushions
swing. There's popcorn if you want some.
I have these tears all over me from when you picked me up
in your jaws. I don't have patience for plot.
Your tears make me uncomfortable. You feel things
and you show that feeling. I have come a long way
to be by your side, and I am almost disappeared.
There is a man on the screen you are always looking at.
We have things in common. This is nice. This would be the best
date if you weren't rehearsing how to leave. No one thinks
they are in a tragedy until they notice where the laughter should be.

BOOK OF JANUS

I have seen a man and a woman sewn together
his arm to hers her spine to his
                 and from behind the one-way glass
which is to them a blind end
I watch them struggle against a red thread
the closeness of skin to skin
and the unbearable sense of trap of constrict of that
which makes the fox gnaw
at his black paw snared in the metal noose.
She had been reaching for a can of tomatoes
when from behind her knee the needle
                 whipstitched her leg to his.
He had been watching his daughter slide
down the slide
when the slip of the thread pulled him across
Texas Wyoming her body
like an America.
                That's how they'll tell it
when they tell it to others
           who bear similar marks
           from the tatting of thread.
I have seen them together straining
against their together all together
        and the woman thinks if she can just get him face to face
        they might talk this away
        and the man wants to run but his legs are hers
they are one body at war with the one war we're all in
together all together we're in.

VOW

They were not traditionalists.
They could bear the innovations
                of plot. They could not
wait to landscape the plot. They had plans
                        for a bed of pansies because pansies
                hardly ever die
                                in a cold snap,
                because pansies are hardy despite the name.
When they shoved the trowel
                        into the soil
it was with his hand
                        on the handle and hers
                                adding force.
They knew there were only
                        nine types of people in the world
and they knew which ones
would close the deal. They knew
the shirkers by sight.
                        They had options.
They knew about Required Communication.
                About how I feel and you feel.
When there was a question
                        of who did the dishes
                        and who did the cat box,
                        it was settled in-house
        and never required an outside contractor.

But the pansies got stem spot, leaf rot, and mildew.
When they looked at their options
                it seemed there weren't really that many
                                        after all.

They swore to uphold the bonds
                    and the principles
                    and the yelling.
They swore to oral sex.
They dressed to the nines and they walked the aisle.
They stood up and received the standard narration.

LOVE POEM FOR WHAT IS

There's nothing in the world that loves you
more than the space you take up.
There's nothing in the world that won't
forget you faster than you forgot
the last person who stepped out of your life.
When the cat reaches up
one needled paw to drag down a book
from your desk, then another,
that's not love—that's dominance.
When you reach out your hand and try to wheedle
someone else's to hold it, that's love
dominating you. There's no word for loving more
than you should, just the feeling of excess,
as if your tongue burst into a rash of red sequins,
as if everyone can see your stutter in the air,
a staccato *love you, love you,* and nothing
in the world standing in that space to receive it.

SLASH FICTION

I want to be your Keanu Reeves

                      when Keanu Reeves is at his most
thespian and anointed, when the big *Whoah*

                      plumes from his lips, which means
the world is a wonder, but the portions are small.

                    I want to be of indeterminate
ethnicity, like him, and so Everyman,

              and I want you to Swayze me
under a pelting rain, all tight shirted

                and defined

                    by both the said and the unsaid,

so that these flimsy lines

        about banks and investigations,

             about honor, integrity, are the closest we can come
to the real of it, to tight jeans and their underpinnings,

            the way we are all constricted
by what we can't say,

        how our mouths won't move
towards the kiss we desire,

                how the building that explodes behind us,
launches us golden and laughing

                  through the blistering air,
           is just a smaller fire.

ELISE AS MARIE ANTOINETTE
AT HER TOILETTE

Come, Léonard, dress my hair, I must go like an actress,
exhibit myself to a public that may hiss me.
—Marie Antoinette to her hairdresser

I dream of a disco heaven,

where Debbie Harry's thin, crystal voice

        arias the sweating bodies into a better

           transcendence,

    where the prettiest boys are sodomatic

        in the strobe, the frozen

cigarette smoke

              and when I open my eyes

it's back to proper powdered skin and the women

        dress and rouge me—

    my microcosm is a sequin on an exquisite shoe

        of which I have ten,

    my day a combed and perfumed lamb.

            Later I will coax an egg

      washed free of context

           from a manicured nest

   in the shape of a straw heart.

I'm not attached to it.

      I put it in the basket with the others.

          It's always the same

             yellow fluff

      that molts into a mother,

        then gets its head cut off

           when the pearls cease

      to descend in an ordered string.

Raise my arms and the cloth cascades.

                  The women arrange me against the light.

        A chemise is not enough freedom,

              the muslin does not reveal

        the body beneath how it vibrates

to the distant syncopated

electric bass the four-on-the-floor beat,

             or the ache I feel to revise the contredanse allemande

       into a hustle

           for the crowd's love—my unwashed darlings

            who could think for a moment I'd deny

you bread cake or anything?

BOOK OF EXCESS

Most of what I loved best I took in pill form,
while sitting
in an Eames chair which is
                    the real deal,
            tattooed
        on a pretty young hipster's forearm,
along with a smiling cupcake, a candy
                        dandy with a cane,
        a pinwheeled
                sucker I'd volunteer
to lick from the outer spiral in—
                        if only.
                In my tattooed state
I flex with her flex, I supple
                when she lounges
on the bed
before her scruffy counterpart,
                whose jeans she can wear
because she is free of hips
                        and he subsists on air
and gold plated stereo cables.
Some days I am a Betty Page
                        and I lean back
across her bicep,
        breasts like bullets and the whip
in my hand.
                Other days I am a Betty Grable,
coy over the shoulder and the legs
                (O those legs)
but always a Betty
                stereo-hyped to an inch of my
life in the public eye in the smoky pool hall in the bedroom
where she and I unbutton her buttons
                and prepare for my big reveal.

ELISE AS ANDROID AT THE JAPAN! CULTURE + HYPERCULTURE FESTIVAL

It takes three men to hoist me
      to the platform, a fourth to hide the cables
           juicing this endeavor,
and during sound check my engineer
           cradles my head, smoothes my hair,
rearranges the folded cloth of my peach kimono,
      tightens the obi with screen printed
           forest scene—
and when he whispers, *You're perfect*, I blush
           as best I'm able,
      and he presses my check, kisses the springy
      cush of my false skin.

At first, the audience is shy, asking me basic questions—
           no compound clauses,
    and I'm witty, I'm a lovely
      hostess, I even tell a joke
           about robots and chickens.
I move in stylized increments, take tiny steps to mimic
    the audience's idea of a geisha,
my white skin
      siliconed to a velvet-cream sheen.
It is all very careful, the awkward
      presented as beauty,
        and I am beautiful, awkward
    as that is.

The crowd grows bolder, the questions more complex:

           Where do you see yourself in five years?
           Why does the mother spider eat her babies?

What's prettier—a girl with a fresh bruise
or a bucket of water?
I stutter, smile.
Can you repeat the question?
They smile back, tight, satisfied.
I'm afraid
I don't understand, I say, again,

and the spectators point
out my hairline as a giveaway,
the sway
when I talk,
shudder at the horror show, her poreless skin, perfect
like a pig's.

BOOK OF THE WILD

I am a wolf, I run
                 to the manicured edge
          of the cul de sac
          in the dark housing development
where there is a guard gate but no wall
                 to keep out those who would rifle and rummage
          through the petunia beds, the blonde wife's silken
                 panties folded in a scented drawer.

I am not really a wolf.
                 I play one on screens that cast a blue glow
onto the snow
          that piles in white laundry and never blackens
with exhaust,
                 though every garage is pregnant
with the beauty of a steel gray Bimmer.
                             Every morning the drifts
                             deepen and threaten the doors,
but all are safe inside.

          This is not an indictment
                 or an exposé of secret sordidness.
They are not sordid.
                 They just like to watch wolves
and see them do wolf things.
                 They watch me den, pup, and play.
When they watch me starve in winter
          the house is warmer for it.

DEAR CHANEL, DEAR ALABAMA, DEAR ELISE

In the mall that is not a mall
                    but a facade of a downtown,
I walk with my wrist drenched in Chanel #5 by an ambitious saleswoman.
The expensive on my wrist
                    has a top note of aldehyde,
                    has a bourgeois drydown.

                    Do I smell like Lauren Bacall
                        in *The Big Sleep*?
No, her slutty sister,
the one who says to Bogie,
                    "You're cute," and passes out.

Around me, smooth-faced men lead their greyhounds in packs
            circling the fountains, everyone sniffing
                            for something familiar.

Such wonders under this scrubbed sky,
        the matrons who are twins to their blonde daughters,
                    the morning mimosa with crepes,
and the evening promise
of Jack Daniels, which once you clutched
                    to your breasts, crowing, *You can take the girl outta Alabama*—

There's nothing left from that night—the bottle emptied,
                            the apartment you stood in, razed—
            your breath champagne and brandy—your skin
                            a perfume I know but don't recognize—
I, too, am prone
        to a dramatic exit, and look best with my caboose
                    swung over a man's shoulder.

NOT HERE TO BUY THE LEOPARD

Today the radishes are colored like a girl's mouth,
and their tops wag from my bag as I walk home,
announcing, *Here is a woman who loves*
a good produce stand, even though I will pull them
from my refrigerator's hydrator in three weeks, faded
and too far gone. Another foolish purchase, as foolish
as the way I attempt to assign personhood to the stuffed
snow leopard in the fancy furniture store on my way home,
the store that believes in the beauty of tiny chandeliers
and taxidermy eyes in a shadowbox. The snow leopard
might not even be a snow leopard, its face stretched,
as if they had a leopard skin but only
a styrofoam puma core in stock.
I do like that it is snarling—simulating snarling—
and every time I come in with my radishes
and my unwashed spinach, the woman behind the counter
bristles. She knows I am here to not buy the leopard.
That night at a party, I overhear
a woman saying there should be a law against hunting
predators, how she hates the hunters who snare and shoot
wolves, for example, and I know she's really thinking
of her two black labs, but the labs are wolves too,
in their cores, just as I am, just like you.

FOX UNDRESSES RABBIT

Think of a summer night,
           insect buzz, golden
               porch light,
                   and let that warmth slide
from your shoulders,

        bare your strap and bear
my weight,
        which is
           fever.
        Maybe I should tell you a story
about how I wake at night with your hair
               still caught in my teeth,
           how nothing can be fixed or fixed.

Think of summer and the jasmine
           opening its waxy petals in the night,
and open a little farther
        your mouth,
           which I'd like to slip
                a finger in,
                which I'd like to see
       mouthing
       the words you promised
           or at least your collarbones
said such things to me,
           led me further afield than I have ever been,
                far beyond the safe confines
                of the measured
                and mapped backyard,
into these dreams I have
           where you are always disrobing,

you drop one kimono, another,
and I never find the heavy breast
my hand was meant to cup, just
more surface, more summer.

ON FIRST SLEEPING WITH ELISE IN THE PRESENCE OF MY EX-HUSBAND

Consider the imperatives.
Drape the leg. Fan the golden
                     hair up a freckled flank, the taut
belly, calculate through juniper, through sloe
                     and the faraway chime
           of ice and highball
how far up the bed to sprawl
to show reticence but not so far
as to avoid touch.
            In the next room
       the party has deteriorated,
what remains is a penchant
           for ironic porn
on the television, for wistful techno
           swayed to
               by stragglers,
     dregs swilling the dregs.

Here, there is a locked door.
Here, there is a man
      standing with full
        awareness, in his hands
a camera
       trained on the two women
             who have the look of desire
if not the exact color of it,
      who are aware of his eyes and their own,
            and once so observed
            are no longer pure
       in their actions,

and who proceed
      with a procedural thoroughness
        and little pleasure,
although there is some pleasure
          after all.

BOOK OF DENIAL

In beginnings there is a pleasure,
                    in the pleasure that begins
there is a beginning unpetaling
                              into thin color slips
                              plastering car windshields,
                              blowing across sidewalks,
where the pedestrians stroll sometimes
                    hand in hand,
                    and in all those tight buds unraveled
there is an order brought low,
          a previous destroyed,
because seeing a lover naked the first time
                                        erases the prior
                                        lover's body of any certainty
                                        in your mind—
          where was that freckle,
          how high the breast—

I cannot remember how he kissed me,
          and though he slapped me
                              when necessary, and in the face
                    when I asked, I can't say anymore
                    the size of his hands or
                              how the peace settled over both of us.
His handprint
                    was beginning to fade
                              as another beginning began,
          begun in the recoil
                    of my head and my smile
in the anteroom
                    of the previous ending,
and if the red thread

I thought linked us abraded, snapped, or just faded,
it also knit into another's,
and then an other's,
so that in this night
that I make new the old is unraveled and respun,
in this night that makes me anew
the old self is made stranger,
how can I
deny her
the requested blow,
that she asked for,
that I asked for?

FOX AND RABBIT WATCH *LA TRAVIATA*

The commentary plays in the cheap seats
                like it plays abroad
because there's a little vulgar
                in all of us
        but it's your vulgar
                        I like best

the way you show your nape
        the way your ankle
                        has no shame
        and you bare your legs
you bare your teeth
                in a smile that seems
                                everyone's
                                property.
You're a small thing,
                barely bigger through opera glasses
but the songs
                you sing

                —I call it singing, that sound
                        you make
                                when I press down—
        are so loud
                they sound the night
with enough light to read
                your fortune by

and because I love
                        a show
        where I have no future

descend the stairs
in whatever costume
you wear best
and let me break down
the door again.

FAIRNESS DOESN'T ENTER IN

The birds follow
                    the birds. They move in a cloud
of shared ambition.
                    The trees sway. There must be wind.
This must be landscape, that boat house
                    and the blue lake
                              flapping behind it.
These cars
and the drivers gliding along,
                    also, landscape,
also my body
          walking between the street's bluster,
                    and the postcard's script.

It's not rational
to tint the world
          with shook-out sadness.
Enough sheer layers of color,
                    and you've got real depth.
There are ducks
          now in the thawed lake.
Small, green tips
          force the ground apart,
shove shoulder
          and then a lemon yellow head.
Color is its own belief.
Everything has reappeared, and what else
          to call it—everything has come back,
but differently, but different.

ELISE QUA ELISE

1

In the beginning
    there was willingness
and there was a long summer
     turning the black paint on the fire escape
       to tar sucking at our shoes
     in a greedy love, *don't go, don't go,*
   and the roofs turned the rare rain
          to steam,
      to air again,
and there was no meaning in any of it, just the ordinary
    prayers and hands,
       just songbirds competing
    with traffic noise,
and her, standing in my doorway,
     telling me how my life
        was no longer solely mine,
how sometimes skin and skin and the air through lips
      bring us to each other
    in one form, to form another,

and to have no quarrel with her
   but with God
   or whomever.

That summer the city was parched,
    the lake low on the boats and the gardens abandoned
      to what could grow without care or love
      except for the secret tendings
      of illegal sprinklers in the dark hours,
and in that summer the few trees outside

our apartment complex were still
and a blight took them out
and then a chainsaw.

2

When I said my life, I meant my husband
how she wifed him one night
after a party I'd left early.
Despite this new information,
history and the greater world
continued, the first plane
hit and the radio announcers jabbered
confusion, a mistake, a freak
accident but then it wasn't
and we watched the live feed
of one body,
two, darting through the smoke to the ground below.
Later, we would try to cast the memory
from a mold of acceptable rhetoric, from received sources,
from cooler heads, the moment
never replayed
because the bodies had families
and the bodies had carried in them something
other than body
and if we didn't name it
we could avoid mistaking it.

3

In her mouth
a mistake

took wing, the brandy and champagne
                    channelled down
her arm, crested one breast, and we listened to the rattling
                    call of buildings under threat,
progressed
through the colors
of alarm, took our shoes
                    off and passed through
                        invisible rays,
let strangers press our underwires
                    for hidden sharps,
for months
to years until the fear felt earned.
I divorced. She married.
There were postcards,
then there weren't, there was talk
                    of arrest and there was talk
of drugs and then there was no talk.

Across the rooftops the curls of vapor.
Across the smoke the silhouettes falling.
                    The birds against the mechanical.
                    The mechanical bird against the flat gray.

So she said it was a mistake, our bodies'
                    collision, no different
from other accidents, and so I said
                    it was a mistake, our bodies'
                collision, and in other years
                there were other accidents,
                and we each put a footnote
                at the bottom of the history.

4

The problem with a history is the memory
won't square, the house leans
            to one side with the pressure
of ghosts, and all the rats
                flood out,
      breaking the drought
                    with their rolling bodies.
There was no great love
              between us. I'll never know
if the body she was in held the brighter thing
         I looked for,
                but I doubt it.

One summer, another, ended with dark descending
         and all through the parks the fireflies
synchronized, though one man giving another man
        relief by the empty swingsets hardly noticed,
             though a roman candle
spattering in the hands
           of a drunk and laughing girl running
       lit nothing out of the ordinary
          and sputtered out, leaving
only the same stars
         in the same patterns as before
among them the red lights
            of travelers sleeping
with only slight fear
       far above, and her below

                       the earth somewhere

I've never visited, her name

                 returned to her at last

from the mouths of others

                 who passed it back and forth,

fraying its edges,

                      myself among them.

BOOK OF MERCY

Some were blinded, but one broke through the branches
and the bracken, tracking what he thought
was a hare, and found a woman instead, or the shape
of a woman, bathing herself in the stream, long hair a wet rope

down her back,
her hand, rough from the bow's waxed sinew,
cupping one breast, alarmed. He fastened on this scene
as intently as his mouth's phantom tug—

      I'm sorry to say it doesn't end well,
that longing, the story.
                Like him, I have been a hunter of small things
and been surprised by divinity.
                        It is as vast and hopeless
                                as you've heard.
One day I walked on two feet,
the next I was pursued
by the sleek hounds
                I'd cared for, plucked of tick and burr.

                I was supposed
                        to be grateful
                  for the choice to run
            or just hunker down, praying
                what scented me wouldn't also destroy.

TINHEART, LIONHEART,
STRAWMAN, YOU

Morning and all is forgotten.
    The red flags
        are just petals again,
            the shower leaves you pink
    and scented,
    and the day plays forward once more,
            inexorable, unkind.

I'd have you stay a man forever
        crossing from bed to shower,
rather than let evening come
            again
    with its field encircling me,
the red poppies black in the blue light,
        your face not the face I know.

    Home is a dream
        where they wake you back to yourself,
grudging, grateful in the familiar once more,

    and it is familiar,
        this fear, the animal scent
    as you track my steps
on all fours,
        faster without that
troublesome trouble you kept in your chest,
        and without it

        there is room for the judgment
that finds me wanting,

and when you find me,
it's wanting that undoes me,
                picks me up
and sets me down
in a fragile, teacup world
            and I break the handle off.

FOX DRESSES RABBIT

This is better.
        When I cut off your feet
it's better,
      when I cut off your head
        I feel better,
when my hands are inside you
        it's warm,
what you hid from me,
        these skinned plums,
    these slopping ropes,
          this glisten.
I check for spots.
I am not superstitious.
I have reason to believe
you are sick.
All of that extra matter
      steams on the ground,
but it is a cold day,
    the leaves are brown,
      the sticks crack
under my boot, and the geese overhead
are spelling out words, but I'm not superstitious,
it's just the mind making patterns—

    why have you gone so still?
There's a gold light
    I'm looking for and I know it's further in,
I might keep one of your feet
      for under my pillow.
I want to dream of the one I'll marry and see how she runs.
You can get a good sense
of a relationship

if you consider gait and stride.
Your ears lie so flat against your head.
Do you hear me
even a little?
I sing as I work.
I like to work with my hands.
Are these hands?
They are holding the thing
I wanted.
It looks smaller.
It looks better smaller.

REVISION: ELISE

In one story you wash up
on a cold shore, your blue lips parted
                  around hidden pleasures—
and even sodden, scrubbed by salt, cocooned in thick plastic,
you blonde and you starlet.

It's my hope that a handsome agent of the FBI
will investigate your death,
             determine its mystical origin,
but until then, the real story:
you just didn't wake up.

There are many ways to die,
but I thought yours would be in a Daimler,
practicing an aria
just before your cream cashmere scarf
spooled around a tire, winching you into the sunset.

Or maybe you are covered in gold leaf
and suffocated
quite prettily,
        face down,
        your bottom shining like a good idea,
because we breathe
           through our skin, or no,

we live because our skin
might one day be accessed
by a spy's methodical hand.
No amount of excess
        beauty can make up
           for that hand's withdrawal.

Let us be naked in every way,
and when the story's end asks for you
               let's say you were only kidding.
Part your mouth again, and let a measure slip
               like a kimono off your shoulder,
cross and uncross your heart
        with plain-speech integrity,
and hope not to die.

BOOK OF LETTING GO

I was as white as chalk could make me,

                                pure as an assumption,

and I stepped towards you, bare feet spread wide

                    on the leaves, belled at each ankle.

Still you didn't hear me.

                    So I stepped as a doe picks her way,

                    as if the ground might open,

                    as if every tree housed a hunter

                    in its canopy,

          and you dreamed on.

You were wounded

          and I tied a scarf around your mouth

          to keep you quiet,

                  I bound your chest

                with rope to keep you safe.

I pulled you behind me

and the leaves

parted like a green sea,

                the trees awakened

                    in the wake,

          and you were light, my love.

          You were no hard thing.

                        You were a chiming in my walk,

                    you were a sound that carried

                        itself over and over the trees.

But what knots I made were slip.

The tug of passage picked each one open,

          free of my bindings your heart could beat,

          your wounds could seep,

and your gag

     —it was a gag—

came loose

and you started to sing

a song for someone not me,

and it followed my feet as they sank in the mud, the green

waves that muted my bells,

the body I carried behind me,

    your body

      laughing and pointing behind me.

ELISE IS NOT ATLANTA OR ATALANTA

She's not a gate left unlatched.
The garden is not one
                where the tree branches brush the ground
because the fruit is so heavy,
              and she's not that rotting sweetness
              or that fermented juice,
              she's not the monkeys
pawing it to their mouths
                  or their drunken stumbling after.
She is not a golden apple
                or the lust for possession.
She's not the foot race that ends with her married off,
              and she's not the lion skin she wears
because proper thanks were forgotten.
                    She thanks.
                    She thanks the wedding guests
                    who brought so many presents.
The vacuum that never loses suction.
The immersion blender.
The golden apple rolling down the aisle.
The ships
that crowd the shore.
The men
who tear her away
and the man who tosses her over one broad shoulder.
She is not the beauty this implies.
              She's not a face that slips
                  the ships from dock.
She doesn't race after an apple
              for knowledge but would to forget.
              She does not apple, ever.
She's not Peachtree Street or Peachtree Street or Peachtree Street.

She's not the Majestic
                    serving food that pleases.
She does not please.

FIRST HUSBAND

I took you in your blue Walmart vest, took your may I help you
literally, took the keys to your car and threw them out the window.

I took thee to the prom. I took your best friend for a test drive,
but we were on a break. I took you stupefied

by misapplied Prozac, I took the part of Ingénue #2
to your experience, sat with welted ass and demure face, blushing

over my bound wrists. I took your shaved curls from the sink,
and they clung to me. I took your love and called it crush.

I took you seriously and got took. I took my itinerary
across the southern states and folded the map until we overlapped.

I took the vodka bottle from your hand and poured it over my breasts.
I took your clothes that smelled like her and stuffed them

in the litter box. I took my cues from what I thought I should feel
in the role of Betrayed Wife, or Betraying Wife, or Wife Who Can't

Remember Who Fucked Who Anymore. No more ingénue.
I took your hand one last time. I took down your new address.

I took your hand again. I took my tongue and
touched it to your lips, but you wouldn't kiss me.

I took that as no but knew what no meant to us,
so I took your pants off, I took no excuses,

Michael, I took your name, I took your hand,
and in the perpetual backward glance, I take your name again.

FOX ASSESSES RABBIT'S DAMAGE

All those weeks I slept outside your door
                        in a sack
                        made of hair,
            you never noticed
        my carbon footprint,
        my impact on the flowerbed,
how I went through
such changes there,
                how I waxed and waned
        to the width of your silhouette
                        against the glow
            of another man's
                        possessions.

In the lessening winter light I inserted
a pencil in your bedroom window frame,
                        to keep it open
                        just enough.
You slept on, and in that sleep
                you were always saying
                        wrong things.
                That was my fault.
There were many ways of making you talk,
                but my favorite was to slide my hand
                        under your shirt
            and work your mouth around
the thick of it.

            Language
should be keyed
                        to the beauty of the speaker,
        that is, ugly

as life has marked you,
                              lithe
            as the lie you need.

These days I try to sleep
                  like a man, in a bed, my own.
I am my own man
                        even if only my hands
            register the condition.
                  Didn't these hands
                              once have the measure
                                          of how far
                  you could stray
from an ideal
                  woman's face?

I sleep in my own bed.
I call it sleep even when I wake
to the same room.
But when I change the sheets
I find your hairpins, your books,
I find you
folded
under the mattress.

Who then did I watch
                  for so long and why
was she a prettier thing?
                              You are dried and withered.
                              You are not what I thought.
I liked the other one, how she looked
against the light, the distance of her.
Sometimes I shook the window and she fell to the ground.

YOU ARE THE PENULTIMATE
LOVE OF MY LIFE

I want to spend a lot but not all of my years with you.
We'll talk about kids
                    but make plans to travel.
I will remember your eyes
                    as green when they were gray.
Our dogs will be named For Now and Mostly.
            Sex will be good but next door's will sound better.

There will be small things.
I will pick up your damp towel from the bed,
                            and then I won't.
I won't be as hot as I was
                    when I wasn't yours
and your hairline now so
            untrustworthy.
When we pull up alongside a cattle car
            and hear the frightened lows,
            I will silently judge you
            for not immediately renouncing meat.
You will bring me wine
            and notice how much I drink.

                The garden you plant and I plant
            is tunneled through by voles,
                    the vowels
                    we speak aren't vows,
        but there's something
            holding me here, for now,
        like your eyes, which I suppose
                    are brown, after all.

BOOK OF FORGET

I made a stage out of an abandoned house, small
enough for me to look bigger, and I walked from end
to end in spangles, shaking what my momma
gave me in a symphony jiggling over the dry
desert night. I danced after the knife thrower threw
his blades and before the velvet clown kicked away
his chair and hanged himself, his tongue thick and purple,
urine dribbling down to the boards. There were
men in the audience, their hands hidden,
but mostly the darkness around me was oily
and the floods pooled no farther than the music
carried. Once a woman came and sat in the front row,
wife to a husband who stayed overlong in my dressing room.
She watched my entire act. I hope she went away
with some kind of answer. These steps remain
the same regardless who watches: one two, and I turn,
three four, I cock the hip. I wanted to be a contortionist,
to stand on my own neck before anyone else could,
but the world is full of women who can halve themselves.
My talent is in looking like someone you want
when the lights are up and like anyone who'll do when they're down.
There are other ways to dance, but I never learned.
There are other ways to forget. This one will suffice.

SPRINGTIME, ELISE, AND YOU'RE MISSING ALL OF IT

Not the expected robin, or the ragged deer
        stepping from the woods
                to lip the new green—

but the girls in bikinis who stand
                in Tallahassee traffic, waving Car Wash signs,
                their pert behinds a greater glory
than pollen count, or
                even gravity.

                      Boxing ring girls, sans spangles,
        they leg in heels from corner to corner,
the culmination of suffragettes
                and Betty Friedan, their every step

a violin's reel in the orchestra
                of the sunny day, a glare
        that makes me lower my shades
                against it all.

                You'd say it was a word
                      like *heartbreaking*—
how in the coffee shop
        the young man's shirt is open just enough
        to see a flash
                of curling hair—

Either that or *tasty*—

        Let me put it another way—

even though you're not sitting here,

                the bored policemen direct traffic,

          the strolling dogs sniff from ass to ass,

the telephones still ring.

FOOL'S JOURNEY

There's a dog that nips at my heels
                    like a moral lesson,
and on days I am closest to the cliff's edge
                I think the dog
might be warning me, but it's hard
                  to tell if he wants to use his sharp teeth
        to pull me back
            at the last instant,
        or if he means to drive me farther and over, so I hang
for a moment in the air,
                then fall through the donut smoke
                              of my own
                              surprise.

It's helpful to see my animal nature
        so clearly, and to know
                it's a terrier, vicious and unrelenting.
                        It has no collar or master.
I'm not blind to danger,
            I just can't tell
whether it's the space beyond
           that destroys me, or the ground
I walk along,
        all I own in the world on my back, singing.

BOOK OF GHOSTS

Imagine roses here. Imagine red lips around a central bud.
Sere grasses shot through with green again, the rock garden's boulders
wearing soft moss cauls. Imagine a peacock high stepping
across the little creek. Imagine the little creek
unfrozen. Small minnow dart and duckweed bloom.
    A memory of how things should be.
    A memory of things, being.
All sewn with gold thread to the cold packed ground.
This season it's short skirts and highballs, the next—

we pull away from what sustains us. I am not accountable
for the earth's yaw, the inconstant love
        of light. I tilt my cheek
so far the kiss can't land. This is called veering.
Imagine veering through the botanical gardens
        in winter light, drunk
on hot brandy, the falling snow's indifference
to moderation, indifference to the injured goose
that has lain down in the white. It hisses, tucks its beak
under the broken wing.
    I look away from it, its damage. I veer.
The stars are clearer when indirectly viewed.
Bright the way my tongue presses forward
   against my teeth, as if to latch
    to a thick dark nipple—that hunger—
     O, the things we want.

MY ANSWER TO YOU IS YES (FORMERLY NO)

In the garden I was building
based on courthouse records
     transcripts
     photographs
     and letters
there were a lot of trees
that had a lot of significance
          but I didn't install choice.
The world was more of a set
        piece for me
        to rabbit around in.
I put you in a fox suit
but the fit was tight so I put you
     in a box and labeled it fox
but you split the sides and lounged out.

I have sent you letters but I couldn't hold a pen
     so mostly I sent you blank and undrafted and mostly
          I sent you
          nothing.
I have been in a burrow
     which is not
        a home
I have been in a home and heard your scratch
at the door and watched as the dirt
        caved in.
Without your face
     blocking out the light
I can't know where the hope was.
Won't you
     please
     please chase me goddamnit.

GOLD EMPIRE

This is the world
                we get and only this
          the blood and the water mingle
and wordless
          the moan among lilies and honeysuckle
the branches shake
              like my arms after rough
          sex I want
                  you fresh from the hunt
your face smeared with the perfume
              I leave on your mouth
          it's this overgrowth that reminds me
              of how much
          we are overrun
                  with excess and the lush
I have pressed
          this hand to your plush

                  forget
          that I said this.
          This world
              we made is the only one we get

          and it splays to a golden
center
              and it singles us out
for sacrifice.

ELISE, YOUR PHONE IS RINGING

If this is a poem about loss
        then let's mention your cell phone
dropped into the high grass
        in front of a boarded up house
        between Little Five Points
        and Candler Park
        in the Atlanta
which is always under revision
from drug dealer domicile
to gentrified bungalow
only to peel and chip back
        to the low rent and then the abandoned
like the antique windows
        salvaged by graphic designers
        still hanging from chains on the porches
their cathedral glass casting ruby red
        splash across the warping wood
        in the light of a flickering street lamp.

Your phone only missed
after palmed painkillers
after casting eyes at the waiter
after paying the bill in the agonies
        of drunken math.
You led a pack of women down the sidewalk
        all of us calling out, *Elise! Elise!*
        to our own phones
        to the heat laden night
        to the flat gray light polluted cosmos
        and the kudzu slumping green monsters above us
        as the cicadas all thrummed
to drown out the ring

of the small Samsung red flip phone
            we rang and rang again.
Elise! Elise! We are stumbling to find your voice
            amongst cigarette butts and crushed coffee cups
                        amongst PBR carcasses and lotto tickets.
We are pilgrims in our seersucker dresses
                                    Hosannah Hosannah
and we are palms out
            we are clicking and clacking
in our prayer beads looping between our breasts
            we are high heels tripping
we are perfume
            smearing the night into artificial bloom
and when we hear your phone's trilling tones
            we scream triumphant
            we paw the grass
            we find it
            grasp it
            your hand clasps mine
            Elise! Elise! pick up.

BOOK OF WATER

Everything begins with a wreck
                    and an upset to order.
The ship runs aground
and a man
pulls himself up
      from the sand.

         The car stops its spin
and rests against
the bridge's guardrail, as if pausing
      to breathe.

As for me
      I was never bound
         to a tree and laughing.

No slick words held me nor the spelling
            of his name
a fathom below and a peeling pearl above
         the grit against my teeth a certainty.

I was tied to the earth
         as we all are tied,
      by root and by obligation

by a promise to hold
fast and a ceremony
where the feet
sequence a sentence that ties
         one to another's traced back

as we all are tied to the steps of those prior

to the instance in the moment in the year.

The story of she loves and he
                    where no
                    monster might sunder
no father might meddle

no spirit part
the tree branches and speak
                    to the right or the wrong—

that story
has no guarantee. If she loves and he
then the car can still glide
                    across the icy highway
like a ship in a certain storm
all beyond the acts
of a man's steering.

Let us recognize
          how in the moment against the precipice
there is respite and respiration,

how when I ask for release
                    from the bondage
I've asked for
          to be applauded
                    from this island at last

order descends
                    again
like a heavy cloak
                    over an old man's shoulders.

LOVE POEM FOR WHAT WASN'T

I am the woman looking over one shoulder,
                bent over a matte black piano,
composing with my spirit hand,
            and sometimes when I speak a white fluid
seeps, spins and clumps
        in the air above me,
sometimes there is evidence
       of an afterlife,
                  sometimes there is only hoax.

Just as the back of a girl's neck
              and the wisping strays
       call to your lips
         like sacrament,
         so too there is a crash
              that shakes the chandelier
      and sends light chaotic through the room,
    an increasing rapping
    that denies even this
         small grace, taste, and the hand on the page
         takes up the pen,
         and circles and circles *no*,
           writes *I am so fucked* brighter and
           brighter—

A woman desired
     passes hand to hand like a folio,
           marked and corrected,
     marking and correcting, revised, canonized, until beatific in
     beauty—
if I couldn't be her
     I'd be stranger,

if I couldn't be loved
I couldn't haunt you like a house left open,
the beds unmade,
blur my edges until my face
grows obscure but my perfume remains,
smoky like a campsite abandoned
and the rain hissing the fire to sleep—

this is my anger at my own fear
of mercy.
This is not my speaking voice, but a shiver passing through,
the birds that rise in the frame of my window,
crossing and recrossing,
have a word for this
but my hand can't trace the letters.
This will have to do.

NOTES

"Slash Fiction" owes any beauty it may have to the movie *Point Break*.

"Fox and Rabbit Go to the Movies" references the opening scene of the movie *Get Low*.

"Elise as Android at the Japan! Culture + Hyperculture Festival" was inspired by Actroid-DER2, an android who answered questions posed to her by attendees of the Japan! Culture + Hyperculture Festival in 2008.

"Questions About the Wife" is for Matt Guenette, and was written at his behest.

"Love Poem for What Wasn't" draws inspiration from the Fox Sisters.